100
GREAT
INDIAN
POEMS

100 GREAT INDIAN POEMS

Edited by

Abhay K.

B L O O M S B U R Y

NEW DELHI • LONDON • OXFORD • NEW YORK • SYDNEY

BLOOMSBURY INDIA
Bloomsbury Publishing India Pvt Ltd
Second Floor, LSC Building No. 4, DDA Complex, Pocket C – 6 & 7,
Vasant Kunj, New Delhi 110070

BLOOMSBURY, BLOOMSBURY INDIA and the Diana logo are trademarks of Bloomsbury Publishing Plc

First published 2018

Disclaimer: The editor's views are his own. The views expressed by the contributors in this anthology are solely their own. The editor is not liable or responsible for their views.

ISBN: 978-93-86950-93-2

2 4 6 8 10 9 7 5 3 1

Printed and bound in India by Replika Press Pvt Ltd

To find out more about our authors and books
visit www.bloomsbury.com and sign up for our newsletters

This homage we pay
to the great writers of yore;
our own language too
we adore:
an immortal part
of our soul.

Uttararāmacarita of Bhavabhūti 1.1

CONTENTS

EDITOR'S NOTE

On 10 December 1950, William Faulkner began his Nobel Prize acceptance speech with these words, "I feel that this award was not made to me as a man, but to my work – a life's work in the agony and sweat of the human spirit, not for glory and least of all for profit…"

As art transcends the artist, poetry transcends the poet. Faulkner further elaborated upon the importance of artwork over the artist in an interview with *The Paris Review* in 1956. Referring to the futility of conflict over the authorship of Shakespeare's works, he contends, "…what is important is *Hamlet* and *A Midsummer Night's Dream*, not who wrote them, but that somebody did. The artist is of no importance. Only what he creates is important."

This is what I had in mind when I started editing *100 Great Indian Poems* and its companion volume *100 More Great Indian Poems*. The poetry anthologies I have come across have a clear emphasis on 'the poets,' illustrated in the titles such as *Ten Twentieth Century Indian Poets*, *Twelve Modern Indian Poets*, *Nine Indian Women Poets* or *60 Indian Poets*. *These My Words*, edited by Eunice de Souza and Melanie Silgardo, which could be otherwise daunting and inaccessible to common people, may be an exception. These lines from De Souza's poem 'Meeting Poets' are telling –

I am disconcerted sometimes
by the colour of their socks
the suspicion of a wig
the wasp in the voice
and an air, sometimes, of dankness.
Best to meet in poems:
cool speckled shells
in which one hears
a sad but distant sea

A general reader does not need to know which prizes a poet has won, how many books has s/he published or which festivals has s/he attended; the charm and force of an individual poem is sufficient to move the reader. Poetry survives the poets because of its timeless and intrinsic value. Therefore, I don't understand the obsession of the 20th century anthologists of Indian poetry with the poets.

I was fascinated with *Rashmirathi* by Ramdhari Singh Dinkar while growing up as a child in Bihar. I chanced upon my father's worn-out copy of this book at home when I was in class four. The magic that I had felt in the sound and energy of words in *Rashmirathi* stays with me till date. This Hindi epic tells the story of Karna, Krishna, Pandavas and Kauravas. It was my first lesson in literature as well as in politics and diplomacy. I memorised the third canto by heart as I often read it. I still do. I have unsuccessfully tried to translate this work into English. The magic of native words is lost in translation; and therefore, verses from *Rashmirathi* do not find a place in the anthology of great Indian poems. For the similar reason of untranslatability, several other great poems could not fit into this anthology.

Editing *100 Great Indian Poems* has been a labour of love for me. I have read widely, almost all poetry anthologies which have been published so far, covering different languages and geographical regions of India. This anthology includes poems from 28 Indian languages, viz., Assamese, Bengali, Bhili, Dogri, English, Gondi, Gujarati, Hindi, Kannada, Kashmiri, Khasi, Kokborok, Konkani, Maithili, Malayalam, Marathi, Nepali, Oriya, Persian, Punjabi, Rajasthani, Sanskrit, Santhali, Sindhi, Tamil, Telugu, Urdu and Prakrit languages including Pali. The canvas of this collection strives to cover over 3000 years of Indian poetry. Interestingly, along with many well-known names, some poets whose great poems are included in the anthology are virtually unknown even in poetry circles. Poems included in this anthology have shades of all *rasas* (which roughly translates as flavours) including erotic, comic, heroic, horrific among other strains and cover almost all traditions of Indian poetry including *bhakti* poetry. The distinctive voices of the tribal, dalit, feminist and LGBT communities also find space in this collection.

My purpose of editing *100 Great Indian Poems* is to take great Indian poems to the world. This was called for after having brought some of the world's best poems to India in *CAPITALS* in 2017. The present anthology of Indian poetry and its companion *100 More Great Indian Poems* have been transcreated into Irish by Gabriel Rosenstock.

The Portuguese, German, Greek and Spanish editions of *100 Great Indian Poems* are also in progress.

What makes a poem great? Is there a standard definition of a great poem? I have a simple answer to this question. What moves me is great for me. It could be a painting, a piece of music, a photograph, a poem or anything under the sun. I don't think there is or there can be a universal definition of greatness. Even Buddha, the enlightened one, advised his followers not to believe what he said without verifying it themselves, not to take his path but to find one's own. In a similar vein, I would suggest you find your own poems. Make your own anthologies.

This anthology opens with an ancient verse by Bhavabhuti, which, looking over its shoulder, remembers the achievements of past masters but not without offering homage to the language – the vehicle of poetic spirit all over the world. May poetry live on, and languages thrive in our troubled world.

The poems in this collection are arranged in alphabetic order of their respective titles instead of the chronological dates of publication, so as to underline the timeless nature of great poetry. There are a number of great poems I could not include because of my inability to get permissions. These include 'Self Portrait' by A.K. Ramanujan, 'Station Dog' by Arun Kolatkar, 'Night of the Scorpion' by Nissim Ezekiel, 'Postcard from Kashmir' by Agha Shahid Ali, 'The Vaiyai Poems' from Paripatal, 'Indigo' by Chitra Banerjee Divakaruni, 'One Chooses a Language' by Zulfikar Ghose, *Bhagavad Gita*'s Chapter IX translated by Stephen Mitchell, 'In the Cemetery' by Karaikkal Ammaiyar, 'Whatever wound a man inflicts on a woman' by Vatsyayana, 'Woman' by Hira Bhansode, 'The First Book' by Amrita Pritam, 'Fear of Death' by Bhartrihari among others.

I read these poems again and again, in times of joy and sorrow; and while reading these, I enter into a world of bliss. I wish you too an unforgettable journey with these *100 Great Indian Poems*.

Abhay K.

A POEM

– Mir Taqi Mir

Love brings tiny sweat into your hair
like stars marching in the dead of night.

Joy fills my eyes, remembering your hair, with tears,
	and these tears roll and shine;
Into my thoughts is woven a dark night with raindrops
	and the rolling and shining of love songs.

Translated from Urdu by E. Powys Mathers

A POEM NEVER SAYS ANYTHING

– Uttaran Chaudhuri

A poem never says anything.
It just opens a door, quietly.

Sleepless and bent
just like my aged father
waiting for me in a lonely winter night.

Translated from Bengali by the poet

AMBAPALI

–Vishwanath Prasad Tiwari

This dense leafy mango grove
fragrant with new blossom
is not real – it will not last Ambapali
That's what Tathagat had said.
These leaves, green like parakeet feathers
shall fall,
bare branches will wither
Birds shall no longer be drawn here –
Tathagat had said.
Ambapali looks in the mirror
and asks of her gorgeous eyes, bright as gems –
She asks of her tender curls, black as swarm of bees
She asks of her arched eyebrows,
She asks of her fragrant, ornament-adorned body
She asks the trembling desires on her lips,
She asks the glowing embers of her being –
Asks Ambapali –
Can't these words of the truthful Tathagat
not be otherwise?

Ambapali: A famous royal courtesan of the Vaishali Republic in India around 500 BCE.
Tathagat: The honorific title by which Buddha is addressed.

Translated from Hindi by Sunita Jain

AMRUTLAL

– Udayan Thakker

With green ink, sometimes with red
Amrutlal would write down his poems
very carefully, in neat handwriting
in his leather-bound diary
Sometimes he had this terrible nightmare
that he died of the plague
that after his death his poems
were never published
not even found
But Amrutlal lived a long life
(He was my friend)
During his lifetime he saw
the birth of his "Collection of Poems"
He also saw it age
and die.

Amrutlal: Someone who is immortal

Translated from Gujarati by the poet.

AUBADE

– Jayshankar Prasad

Awake for the night is spent.
In the well of the sky the dawn
dips her vessel of stars
to the sound of birds at their morning-song.
The young leaves
are a veil, swaying.
How soft along the vine are the buds of Spring!

Awake for the night is spent.
Your lips hold life in a stillness;
your hair entraps the south-wind.
Ah, you are asleep with the night-song filling your eyes!
Awake. The night is spent.

Translated from Hindi by Romila Thapar

AUBADE

– R. Parthasarathy

You wake up and slip quietly out of the room,
shutting the door behind you. Eyes closed,
I clasp your pillow in hopes of smelling out
the faintest trace of your body's secret perfume.

Never before have I held you more closely
than I hold you now in your absence,
but you hug the morning paper to your chest
in the kitchen and wash it down with a cup of tea.

English

BARS

– Keki N. Daruwalla

If you want
a cage, my dear
you do not have
to travel far.
If you want to feel
hemmed in,
you'll be hemmed in.
Look for scars
you'll be full of scars.
Even light can turn
into a cage.
The cage of light
has seven bars.

English

BLACK BAG

– Pavankumar Jain

I have a desire
To put an end to my life,
But not today,
There's nothing special
About today.

Moreover,
I have two glass bottles to clean,
A haircut to get,
My cataracts operated,
Plants to water
(They're flowering at the moment),
A younger sister to look after.
And I haven't stopped dreaming of the stranger
Who'll leave me his millions.

For now I'll put
The talk of death
In my tattered black shopping bag
Full of holes
And hang it from a nail
In the wall.

To be honest,
I'd like to become a sadhu.
But it'll be years before I can bring
Any sort of order to the chaos
That surrounds me.
There's also the awkwardness
Of moving around in a loincloth,
Begging for alms.
That's one thing.

Then, there are the mothers
Who'll want to scare their little ones
By pointing at us:
There goes a sadhu.
He's come to catch you.
It's not easy to get used to all this.

Best that I put this away too
In my tattered black shopping bag
Full of holes
And hang it from a nail
In the wall.

Translated from Gujarati by Arvind Krishna Mehrotra

BONE OF TIME

– Jayanta Mahapatra

Is this why one always remembers:
the autumn night struggling with its breath,
the fireflies pulsing and drawing back
to reveal the fallen teeth of the forest:
and the moon, to whom we owe
the tempests of light among the shadows,
seeking refuge
in a narrow window of our wakefulness.

The last time I saw you, I told myself:
I would see nothing, never again,
and the evening stars that fall to earth
could make the distance between us no shorter.
Your window looks so warm from here,
and the wind drifts away noiselessly
across the comfortless river: bone of time
that makes each one understand
how night is night; and through it
to enter the kingdom where Orion turns
calm and certain, into neither darkness nor light.

English

BREASTS

– Kutti Revathi

Breasts
are bubbles, rising from marshlands.

As they gently swelled and blossomed
at due season, at Time's edge,
I watched over them in amazement.

Never speaking to anyone else
they are with me always
singing
of quiet sorrow
of love
of ecstasy.

They have never forgotten
to enthuse the seed-beds
of all my changing seasons.

At times of penance
they struggle and strain;
and at the thrust and pull of lust
like the proud ascent of music
they stand erect.

From the press of an embrace
they distil love; from the shock
of childbirth
milk, flowing from blood.

Like two teardrops,
which cannot be wiped away
when love is thwarted,
they fill, and they overflow.

Translated from Tamil by Lakshmi Holmström

BREATH

– Lal Ded

I trapped my breath in the bellows of my throat:
a lamp blazed up inside, showed me who I really was.
I crossed the darkness holding fast to that lamp,
scattering its light-seeds around me as I went.

Translated from Kashmiri by Ranjit Hoskote

CHAMPA

– Katyayani

Champa grew up
among seven brothers

She was as flexible
as the bamboo reed
snakily she disturbed
her father's sleep
became the black shadow
of his dreams
Champa grew up
among seven brothers.

She was pounded
with the paddy
and thrown away
as garbage with the husk.
A parasitic creeper
grew at that spot.
Champa grew up
among seven thorny bushes.
She returned home once more.

Champa, who grew up
among seven brothers, was found
hanging from the roof
of the house.
She was buried in the web
of water hyacinths
a blue lotus appeared there.

Champa returned home once again
to be offered to the gods

when she wilted
she was crushed and burnt.
Her ashes were scattered
over the whole village.
It rained heavily at night
The next day
outside each door
among the wild *nagphani* weeds
alone and unafraid
Champa was seen smiling.

Nagphani: Cactus

Translated from Hindi by Nirupama Dutt

CHILL OUT

– Anon

Busy right now with my precious bamboo flute,
my delicate fingers on the holes.
Darling, can't snuggle you now,
I'm lost fiddling this melodious flute.
Chill out - eat some chilli!
Can't squeeze you right now.
Busy with my precious little bamboo flute,
my delicate fingers on the holes.

Transcreated from Gondi by Gabriel Rosenstock and Abhay K.

CONVERSATION PIECE

– Eunice de Souza

My Portuguese-bred colleague
picked up a clay *shivalingam*
one day and said:
Is this an ashtray?
No, said the salesman.
This is our god.

Shivalingam: The phallus of Lord Shiva worshipped by the Hindus

English

DANCE OF SHIVA

– Hoshang Merchant

By my bed Shiva dances
his left leg over his head
his hair, fire, sacred thread, anklet flying

In my bed
he and I have become a pillar
kneeling at prayer

Difficult to separate god from supplicant
we have flowed into each other
meanwhile the Lord has danced his own round

Making poor, rich
The ancient, young again
And night, day
Cloud, rain

English

DAWN IN WINTER

– Agyeya

Just enough light
for darkness to show
Just enough rain
for silence to sound
Just enough pain to remember
that I have forgotten
I have forgotten...

Translated from Hindi by Lucy Rosenstein

DEATH OF A ROGUE ELEPHANT

– N. N. Kakkad

As the last trumpeting of the rogue
elephant was heard over the foundations
of unfinished houses, he said to himself:

Is the forest far or near?
The darkness and solitude of the dense
forest stains the evening,
but, scattered all around is
the sprawling, unfinished metropolis.

Streets are empty,
infinitely broad, infinitely long
always criss-crossing
only foundations of houses
a row stretching to infinity
somewhere the remembrance of the sea.

The last trumpeting of the rogue
elephant hit by the bullet
slowly dissolved into silence
The blackness of the dusk
sucked that grief dry
along with the evening sky's blood.

I alone...
I alone walk
not knowing why
along the unfinished walls of these houses.

Translated from Malayalam by E.V. Ramakrishnan

DESCRIPTION OF THE MISSING ONE

– Kunwar Narain

Wheatish-complexion, rustic ways,
 on his brow the scar of a wound,
height not under five feet,
 talks as if he has never known grief.

Stutters.
His age? Somewhat more than many thousands of years, he says.
Looks a bit crazed – but isn't.
Has often fallen off heights and got all broken up

Hence, when seen, will look pieced together
like the map of India.

Translated from Hindi by Apurva Narain

DIGAMBARA

– Anitha Thampi

A lone bowstring
I stretch taut
above the endless earth.

Taking in his two hands
this sky's bow
strung tight,
raising it
like time
touching life
possessed by dreams,
with fear,
with intense love,
he holds the bow
targeting infinity
and shoots into the night
millions of stars.

Digambara: Someone whose garment is the sky. It is also a sect of Jainism.

Translated from Malayalam by K. Satchidanandan

EASY, FRIEND

– Kabir

Easy, friend.
What's the big fuss about?

Once dead,
The body that was stuffed with
Kilos of sweets
Is carried out to be burnt,
And the head on which
A bright turban was tied
Is rolled by crows in the dust.
A man with a stick
Will poke the cold ashes
For your bones.

But I'm wasting my time,
Says Kabir.
Even death's bludgeon
About to crush your head
Won't wake you up.

Translated from Hindi by Arvind Krishna Mehrotra

ENGRAVING OF A BISON ON STONE

– Arvind Krishna Mehrotra

The land resists
Because it cannot be
Tempted, or broken
In a chamber. It records,
By carefully shuffling the leaves,
The passage of each storm, rain,
And drought. The land yields
In places, deliberately,
Having learnt warfare from the armies
It fed. The land is of one
Piece and hasn't forgotten
Old miracles: the engraving of a bison
On stone, for instance. The land
Turns up like an unexpected
Visitor and gives refuge, it cannot be
Locked or put away. The land
Cannot sign its name, it cannot die
Because it cannot be buried,
It understands the language,
It speaks in dialect.

English

EPITAPH

– Shakti Chattopadhyay

He gave up none of the world's pleasures;
He was a poet and a scrounge.

Rejoice! said his publishers. The fellow's dead.
At least he won't now turn up threateningly at the office,
Dressed for the evening, demanding his royalties:
The money, you swine, or I'll gut the place.

And so he was laid on the pyre – poet, troublemaker, pauper.

Translated from Bangla by Arvind Krishna Mehrotra

EPITAPH ON MY GRAVESTONE

– Manushya Puthiran

There is
no one here.
You may go.

Translated from Tamil by C.S. Lakshmi and Arundhati Subramaniam

EVERY LAND OUR HOME

– Kaniyan Punkunran

Every land is our home, and every man is one of us.
Good and evil don't flow from others.
Pain and help for pain appear by themselves.
Even death isn't new. We don't rejoice
that life is sweet, nor are we laid waste by grief.
Like a raft swirling in the waters of a deep river
that roars and crashes upon the rocks
in a thunderstorm under skies bruised by lightning,
our life, dear as it is, takes its usual course.
Wise men, who foresee all things, know this.
And so we don't stand in awe of the great,
much less do we hold the small in contempt.

Translated from Tamil by R. Parthasarathy

FAMINE AND AFTER

– Nagarjuna

For days and days the hearth stayed cold, the hand mill quiet
For days and days the one-eyed bitch slept nearby
For days and days lizards paced on the wall
For days and days rats too were miserable

Grain came to the house after many a day
Smoke rose above the courtyard after many a day
The eyes of the household shone after many a day
The crow scratched its feathers after many a day.

Translated from Hindi by Nalini Taneja

FATHER RETURNING HOME
– Dilip Chitre

My father travels on the late evening train
standing among silent commuters
Suburbs slide past his unseeing eyes
His shirt and pants are soggy and his black raincoat
stained with mud and his bag stuffed with books
is falling apart. His eyes dimmed by age
fade homeward through the humid monsoon night
Now I can see him getting off the train
like a word dropped from a long sentence
He hurries across the length of the grey platform,
crosses the railway line, enters the lane
His *chappals* are sticky with mud but he hurries onwards
Home again, I see him drinking weak tea,
eating a stale *chapati*, reading a book.
He goes into the toilet to contemplate
man's estrangement from a man-made world
Coming out he trembles at the sink,
the cold water running over his brown hands,
a few drops cling to the greying hair on his wrists
His sullen children have often refused to share
jokes and secrets with him. He will now go to sleep
listening to the static on the radio, dreaming
of his ancestors and grandchildren, thinking
of nomads entering a subcontinent through a narrow pass.

Chappals: Slippers
Chapati: Indian bread

Translated from Marathi by the poet

FOUR HAIKU AND A TANKA

– K. Ramesh

abandoned dog ...
looking at the face of
every pedestrian

—

power failure…
closing the book
I listen to the rain

—

pause in the traffic
small yellow leaves
cross the road

—

a village in the mountains
a stray dog becomes
our trek guide

—

summer twilight –
a girl steps out
of the house where
birds keep chirping
in a cage

English

FRIEND, THIS IS THE ONLY WAY

– Sachal Sarmast

Friend, this is the only way
to learn the secret way:

Ignore the paths of others,
even the saints' steep trails.

Don't follow.
Don't journey at all.

Rip the veil from your face.

Translated from Sindhi by Ivan M. Granger

GIANT BUILDINGS
– Munibur Rahman

All our lives
we have crawled into the shadow
of giant buildings,
clinging onto the walls.

Buildings were towering peaks
and we were ants
always on the lookout for food.

Skyscrapers loomed in the way
whenever friends came together.

Those buildings grew taller
as we shrank.

At last, one day, we disappeared,
and left nothing behind
but giant buildings.

Transcreated from Urdu by Gabriel Rosenstock and Abhay K.

GRANDFATHER'S PHOTOGRAPH

– Mangalesh Dabral

Grandfather wasn't fond of being photographed
or didn't find the time perhaps
There's just one picture of him
hanging on an old discolored wall
He looks serious and composed
like a cloud heavy with water
All we know of Grandfather is
that he gave alms to beggars
tossed restlessly in his sleep
and made his bed neatly every morning
I was just a kid then
and never noticed his anger or
his ordinariness
Pictures never show your helpless side
Mother used to tell us that
when we fell asleep surrounded
by strange creatures of the night
Grandfather would stay awake inside the picture
I didn't grow as tall as Grandfather
nor as composed or as serious
Still something in me resembles him
An anger like his
an ordinariness
I too walk with my head lowered
and every day see myself
sitting in an empty
picture frame.

Translated from Hindi by Arvind Krishna Mehrotra

HE IS A POET

– Shankar Ramani

He is a poet, solitary and lonely.
Through the window of his ramshackle house
he watches the sky, day and night.
He is completely crazy
Don't call him closer
Nor talk to him;
Don't even look at him;
You never know
when he would throw
on your body
a basketful of pebbles
But if and when his window
turns into the blue sky
the birds from across the horizon
beckon him to the ethereal light.

Translated from Konkani by Damodar Mauzo

HE PROMISED HE'D RETURN TOMORROW

– Vidyapati

He promised he'd return tomorrow.
And I wrote everywhere on my floor:
"Tomorrow."

The morning broke, when they all asked:
Now tell us, when will your "Tomorrow" come?
Tomorrow, Tomorrow, where are you?
I cried and cried, but my Tomorrow never returned!

Vidyapati says: O listen, dear!
Your Tomorrow became a today
with other women.

Translated from Maithali by Azfar Hussain

HORSE PLAY

– K. Ayyappa Paniker

Four gallant horses
galloped forth.
One was white, one was black,
one was red, one was brown.
One had four legs,
the other had three,
the third horse had two,
and the fourth one had only one.
The one-legged horse
said to the others:
the time for dance has come
dear friends,
let's dance on a single hoof.
All of them were in a thrall
and the dance began.
The four-legged horse fainted instantly,
the three-legged slipped and fell,
the two-legged limped and crashed
only the one-legged horse
danced on and on.

Translated from Malayalam by K. Satchidanandan

HOW TO GO TO THE TAO TEMPLE
– K. Satchidanandan

Don't lock the door.
Go lightly like the leaf in the breeze
along the dawn's valley.
If you are too fair,
cover yourself with ash.
If too clever, go half-asleep.
That which is fast
will tire fast:
be slow, slow as stillness.

Be formless like water.
Lie low, don't even try to go up.
Don't go round the deity:
nothingness has no directions,
no front, no back.
Don't call it by name,
its name has no name.
No offerings: empty pots
are easier to carry than full ones.
No prayers too: desires
have no place here.

Speak silently, if speak you must:
like the rock speaking to the trees
and leaves to flowers.
Silence is the sweetest of voices
and Nothingness has
the fairest of colours.
Let none see you coming
and none, going.
Cross the threshold shrunken
like one crossing a river in winter.

You have only a moment here
like the melting snow.

No pride: you are not even formed.
No anger: not even dust
is at your command.
No sorrow: it doesn't alter anything.
Renounce greatness:
there is no other way to be great.
Don't ever use your hands:
They are contemplating
not love, but violence.
Let the fish lie in its water
and the fruit, on its bough.
The soft one shall survive the hard,
like the tongue that survives teeth.
Only the one who does nothing
can do everything.

Go, the unmade idol
awaits you.

Translated from Malayalam by the poet

HOW TO READ A BOOK

– Muddupalani

When you are reading, and you come to a thorn,
pull it out. Use your knowledge
to heal the book. Don't meddle with poets
who make a living out of finding fault.
They're bad news.

Translated from Telugu by Velcheru Narayana Rao and David Shulman

HOW TO TAME A PAIR OF NEW CHAPPALS

– Gopal Honnalgere

don't keep them together
don't allow them to talk to each other
they may form a trade union

don't leave them anytime near
a wall clock, law books, calendar, national flag
gandhi's portrait or newspaper
they may come to know about
independence day, satyagraha,
holidays, working hours, minimum wages and corruption

don't take them to your temple
they may at once come to know you are weak
your god is false and start biting you

don't take them anytime close to your dining table
they may ask for food
or cast their evil eyes on your sumptuous dinner
first use them only for short walks
then gradually increase the distance
they should never know the amount of work they have to do

pull their tight straps loose
let them feel happy
they are growing bigger
smear some old oil on the rough straps
let them feel they are anointed

now they are good subdued labourers
ready to work overtime
for your fat feet

Satyagraha: Exhortation for truth
Chappals: Slippers

English

I HAVE GIVEN BIRTH TO A SON

– Anonymous Bhil mother

Dear sweet sparrow, deliver this message for me:
Tell my father that I have given birth to a son
Tell my mother that I have given birth to a son
Ask my father to give me a new sari
Ask my mother for a multi-colour blouse
Tell my brother that I have a son
Ask him to give me a sari too
Tell my uncle that I have given birth to a son
Ask him to bring me a multi-colour blouse

Sari: A garment worn by Indian women

Translated from Bhili by Abraham Thuruthumalil

IN HER LOVEMAKING SHE GRIEVES

– Gagan Gill

In her lovemaking, she grieves
In her grief, she makes love

In her lovemaking, she gives him a name
The one she gives the name is illusion
Maya, whose desire moves through her sleep

She knows, in the end
whatever name she calls him by
each name will only be an empty space.

Making love, she thinks
she is safe in her oblivion
in her longing, in her selfishness
She doesn't remember that
the one she desires
is just one fistful of bones.
Bones that come out of the crematorium
in just five minutes

Making love, she breathes
in his flesh, his marrow, his soul

Somewhere around here was his soul
Would she find it
in these fistful of bones?

Each time in her fear
she holds him tightly to her
Each time he slips out from her arms

in her lovemaking
in her grief

Translated from Hindi by J.P. Das, Arlene Zide and Madhu B. Joshi

KABARIWALA

– Kavita A. Jindal

Upper Ridge Road, Delhi, 1975

At the door of our second-floor flat he sits on his haunches,
takes out his scales, weighs the bundles of newspapers,
talks more than usual as he places the kilo and half-kilo weights;
he makes my mother suspicious at his chirpiness.

She insists he weighs the papers again; they haggle
over the price he'll pay for seven kilos, how many paise
for each brown glass bottle, how much for each tin can;
and it's only when he hands over some rupees that he says

Next month my cousin or my uncle will come to collect
instead of me; I'm going away.
Going where, we ask; going foreign, he says.
I'm going where there is free love

Where you can be with whomever you want whenever
you want; probably England, that's where I'm going.
Will you be a kabariwala there, I ask.
Don't think so, he replies, packing away his scales.

Onto his young shoulders he hefts the sacks of papers, bottles
and cast-off pans, informing me that in foreign
they don't re-process old things.
He goes down the stairs whistling.

Kabariwala: A scrap dealer or a rag picker

English

KALLI

– Ajmer Rode

Kalli followed me 8 miles
to the market where cattle were traded
or sold like slaves.
Cows goats bullocks camels . . .

Kalli was black beautiful and six
the prime age for a water buffalo.
She was dry. Repelled bulls as if she had
decided not to get pregnant again.

Hard to afford, my father decided
to sell her. Kalli seemed to understand.
She obeyed as I led her
by the steel chain, one end in my hand

the other around her neck.
I was fifteen. Her nervousness was over
soon after we entered the market
where sellers occupied

their given spaces like matrimonials
on a large weekly page.
Kalli sat with no emotion on her face
like an ascetic close to nirvana.

I sat stood walked around like a
neglected calf. No body bought Kalli.
She followed me 8 miles back home
with no questions in her eyes.

I wasn't sure if my father was sad
or glad to see Kalli back. He just
looked at her like a family member
who had missed the train.

Translated from Punjabi by the poet

LAMINATION

– Shefali Debbarma

The Scheduled Tribe certificate
was issued under the seal and signature
of the Sub-Divisional Officer
in the year I was born.
Lest the valuable paper gets soiled
mother kept it safe
in the folds of her favourite garments
within the cane basket.
After a hundred years, today
her favourite garments have worn out,
turned into shreds
white ants have eaten up the cane basket.
Only the Scheduled Tribe certificate still shines
laminated and framed.

Translated from Kokborok by Saroj Chaudhuri

LOVE SONG

– Nirala

I'm a Brahmin's son
But have fallen
for this girl.

A potter's daughter
We've hired to fetch water,
She comes every morning at the crack of dawn.
She's the one I'm after.

Black as a koel,
No curves to her figure,
Of marriageable age
But not yet married.
That's what did it,
and a sigh escaped me.

Her loud knock on the door
Wakes up the house.
No one else knows what's going on.
She takes the water-pot,
The big one, and steps out again,
My eyes following her.
I haven't lost heart.

February 22, 1939

Translated from Hindi by Arvind Krishna Mehrotra

MAGADH

– Srikant Verma

Which way lies the city of Magadh?
Listen, O rider of the horse.
From Magadh I come
And to Magadh
I must return.

Which way shall I turn?
To the North of South?
Or to the East of West?
Lo, there lies Magadh!
And now it is gone!

It was only yesterday
That I had left Magadh behind,
It was only yesterday
That the people of Magadh had said.
Do not leave Magadh
I had given them my word.
That before the Sun rises
I shall be back

And now there is no Magadh.

Aren't you looking for Magadh as well?
Brothers.
This is not the Magadh.
That you have read about in books
This is the Magadh which you
Like me
Have lost forever.

Magadh: An ancient Indian kingdom in southern Bihar where great Maurya and Gupta empires originated and Buddhism and Jainism developed.

Translated from Hindi by Mrinal Pande

MAKING A CHAIR
– Dileep Jhaveri

Making a chair is the most natural thing
and very easy

You can wait for autumn
for every leaf to fall
or you can pluck out leaves one by one
like a crow picking on mouse flesh
Pull down the tree like an elephant uprooting forests
and remove the twigs like a wolf tearing at the tendons
Split it apart like a crocodile the bones
Bore in holes like a woodpecker
Fixing staves in crosses and hammering nails is an ancient art
Make smooth the surface with putty provided by the pulp
Obtain paints from the ancestors of the trees
buried for billions of years to re-emerge through oil wells
Resins from the freshly peeled bark will provide the sheen

Now sit back on the chair set in veranda
and contemplate over the sprouting green of a grass blade
from a crack in the asphalted pavement
Patiently awaiting a forest

Translated from Gujarati by the poet

MARRIED LOVE

– Srinivas Rayaprol

Every evening
I am met at the gate by my wife
her hair in disorder and her dress a mess
from the kitchen
and the girls hang on leaves of the gate
while my ancient car rolls in.
One carries my bag, the other
my lunch basket.
The day's work is over and I am home.
I have forgotten them all day and now
suddenly remember that I must
disappoint them again
for my evening is planned
for a meaningless excursion to the bars.
And the coffee which my wife has served
is cold in my mouth
and the tales the children have brought from school
are dull on my ears.
In spite of my love for them
I must disappoint them again tonight.

English

MOMENT

– Kaifi Azami

Life is the name given to a few moments, and
In but one of those fleeting moments
Two eyes meet eloquently
Looking up from a cup of tea, and
Enter the heart piercingly
And say,
Today do not speak
I'll be silent too
Let's just sit thus
Holding each other's hand
United by this gift of sorrow
Bonded by stirring of emotions.
Who knows if this very moment
Somewhere in distant mountain
The snow at last may start to thaw.

Translated from Urdu by Pavan K. Varma

MONSOON CLOUDS BE MY MESSENGER

– Andal

Monsoon clouds you spread and spread
to hood earth, your torrent slashes
The sky, you shake the honey-heavy blossoms
of Vengadam hill and strew scented petals.
Go tell the dark lord who killed the demon Hiranya
ripping him with paws of fury
that he has robbed me of my bangles.
He must return them to me now.

Whirling clouds you enlarge in anger
and growl across the sky rending it open

with lightening. Spilling honey you tear
flowers, petals spatter like blood on earth.

Go to the fierce lord who roars and mauls
tossing his mane as his paws rip insides out.

Tell him I'm bloodied. He must heal
with long caresses, still me in his thrall.

Engorged with anger
nails extending he kills
plunging wrists in blood

from these very hands I seek
fondling
gather in my swollen ripeness

as spilling nectar
my body's bloodflower
bursts.

Translated from Old Tamil by Priya Sarukkai Chabria

MOTHER TONGUE
– Kedarnath Singh

As ants return to
their nests,
a woodpecker
returns to the wood,
and the airplanes return to the airport
one after another
stretching their wings in the red sky,

O my language,
I return to you,
when my tongue feels
stiff from
remaining silent,
hurting my soul.

Translated from Hindi by Kalpana Singh-Chitnis

MY POEM

– Surjit Patar

My mother could not comprehend my poem
even though it was written in my mother tongue
She merely thought that some sorrow
plagued her son's soul

She wondered
where had this sorrow come from
when she was there all the time
to guard her son's soul

She scanned my poem with care
and exclaimed to herself
'Look, folks look!'
Instead of telling his mother
who gave him birth from her womb
the son chooses to tell his grief to paper

She held the paper to her bosom
hoping perhaps
that this may be the way
to reach out to her sorrowing son.

Translated from Punjabi by Nirupama Dutt

NOT ENTIRELY HIDDEN

from *Cātu* Verses

Not entirely hidden
like the enormous breasts of those Gujarati women,
and not open to view,
like a Tamil woman's breasts
but rather
like the supple, half-uncovered breasts
of a Telugu girl,
neither concealed nor exposed:
that's how a poem should be composed.
Anything else
is a joke.

Translated from Telugu by Velcheru Narayana Rao and David Shulman

O MY FRIENDS

– Mirabai

O my friends,
What can you tell me of Love,
Whose pathways are filled with strangeness?
When you offer the Great One your love,
At the first step your body is crushed.
Next be ready to offer your head as his seat.
Be ready to orbit his lamp like a moth giving in to the light,
To live in the deer as she runs toward the hunter's call,
In the partridge that swallows hot coals for love of the moon,
In the fish that, kept from the sea, happily dies.
Like a bee trapped for life in the closing of the sweet flower,
Mira has offered herself to her Lord.
She says, the single Lotus will swallow you whole.

Transcreated from Rajasthani Hindi by Jane Hirshfield

O SAKHI, THE FLUTE PLAYS IN THE GROVE

– Salabega

O friend, tell me
who plays the flute
in the grove?
The bare trees bloom
at the sound of his flute.
The air stands still.
Stones turn into water.
The Yamuna flows upstream
and the fish seek the shore.
As the bell tinkles slowly,
freeing us from shame,
there's no time left to wear clothes.
Strange! the Rishi loses his poise
and succumbs to love.
The deer chases the tiger.
Says Salabega: I am Muslim by birth
But my heart is
at the feet of Radhakrishna.

Translated from Oriya by Sachidanand Mohanty and Smita Mohanty

PATALIPUTRA

– Patumarattu Mocikiranar

Tell me, did you see him yourself,
or did you hear about it from someone
who had in fact seen him?
I just want to be sure.
May all of Pataliputra, swimming in gold,
where white-tusked elephants splash about
in the Sona River, be yours!
Tell me, again, from whose mouth
did you first hear of my lover's coming?

Pataliputra: Pataliputra, present-day Patna in Bihar, was the legendary capital of the Mauryan (321-185 BCE) and Gupta (320-550 CE) empires. Founded in 490 BCE by Ajatashatru, king of Magadha, it is located at the confluence of the Ganga and Son rivers.

Translated from Tamil by R. Parthasarathy

PATHS
– Salma

Upon the almirah
against the room's walls
between the swirling fan's blades
a bat clashes,
falls, scatters.

But birds, thousands of miles away
fly across the blue of the sky
and the massing of mountains
and have never, so far,
lost their way.

Translated from Tamil by Lakshmi Holmström

PEDRU UNCLE

– Hemant Divate

One by one your limbs turned traitor
Your wooden armchair
The ashtray in which you put out your *bidis*
Your shit-pot
The flutter of your faded Bible
And one frame of Christ is all that remains
I can still feel your presence
lying in the armchair, coughing and moaning
restlessly smoking *bidis*
Your life's becoming intolerable for you
But you can't restlessly
Pace about the room
Your lips tremble
but can't utter a word
Even the smoke trailing out of your *bidi*
seems as paralysed as you

In front of the framed Christ
mentally murmuring a prayer
your whole body is murmuring
Perhaps one last prayer for you and us
You used to ask everybody
'What do you do these days?'
At that time I was doing nothing
except writing poems
You used to say
'You are mad'
But you would read my poems
with great interest
You used to say
'When I was in college
I used to write poems
But that was because of madness

Poetry makes you weak, my son
The day I stopped writing
I stopped worrying about others
And I became the strongest man.'

All your life you were without a companion
All your life you remained an orphan
Nobody ever loved you

And now in a zero watt bulb's light
the words in the Bible must seem very faded
in the same way you too seem faded
to us all

From the bars of your window
you must be seeing
the day turning into night
You must be guessing the time by rough estimate
You can't expect anyone to arrive
And if at all you do wait for something
it is for the window and all the seasons you sense through it
to fall upon you like leaves
And when all by yourself
you would finally remember

your life
Silently
you would pray for Jesus
with an anguished soul
Uncle
You are nobody's relative
Whom will you remember?
And if you remember your life
what exactly was worth remembering in your life?

Now,
when I remember you I feel
I may be toppled down any moment myself

But
I am still holding on
Because I'm mad, Uncle,
I still write poems
I'm mad

Bidi: A cheaper cousin of cigarette made of unprocessed tobacco.

Translated from Marathi by Dilip Chitre

PEOPLE

– Tukaram

The deception was eating into me
so I started calling my dog 'God'.
He thought it was a bit loony
at first,
then he started to laugh, and even
danced a bit of a jig.
'Here God!' – he doesn't bite
any more. Now,
I wonder would
this work
with people?

Translated from Marathi by Anon

PLAY

– Ashok Vajpeyi

I spread out earth's green bed
I pull in sky's blue veil
I place sun and moon on two pillows
I remove grass's attire
I indulge in play with you.

Translated from Hindi by Sudeep Sen

PRAISE GALORE TO THE LAND OF DHAT

—Rangrelo Bithu

The low hills are stony, russet and bare,
with no trees on them save the stunted thorny cactus.
You wouldn't hear the call of a peacock
in all the land.
Hyenas, porcupines and monitor lizards
are the only creatures that you'd come across.
The people are starved;
hunger drives them afield
in search of the prickly grass
whose seeds I have seen them eat.
Such as the Jadavs of Jaisalmer.

The senior queen drives her donkeys
to a distant pond to fetch her water;
alone she must go,
and bestirring with her hands
the water
to clear its surface
of the floating dirt and debris,
fill her pots;
and load them on to the wooden frames
on the donkey's backs
and drive them home,
trudging all the way,
tired and exhausted.

The king's chief bard is pot-bellied;
he wears his lower garment
in a loose unseemly manner;
he is lame in both his legs;
and groans at every step he walks.

The carpet on which the Rawal's court assembles
is worn, with large holes in it;
his poets are all stupid
and cannot distinguish between
a buffalo and an elephant;
to them coarse wool
and silk are just the same.
Such is the land of Dhat!
Praises be to the land of Dhat!

The comely women all go
to fetch water at dawn;
they return past midnight
dishevelled and distraught;
their dishevelled children
pine for them all day.
Such, indeed, is the land of Dhat!
Praises galore to the land of Dhat!

Dhat: heck, surprise

Translated from the Rajasthani by Kesri Singh

PUNDARĪKA

– Kshemendra

When he heard the news of his death
he stood without moving.
Then he let out a piteous cry
loud enough to break the stones of the mountains,
piercing his own life, rendering him unconscious.
O Pundarīka!
Even now, long past, when the deer remember it
they drop the grass from their mouths.

Punadarika: A legendary mythological figure in Hinduism described in *Skanda Purana* as an ascetic and devotee of God Vishnu.

Translated from Sanskrit by W.S. Merwin and J.M. Masson

SELECTIONS FROM *AMARUŚATAKA*

The house parrot overheard
the lovers' sweet nothings
all through the night,
when the sun arose
he spilled the beans;
members of the household
heard every syllable.
When she heard her own sweet words
the woman placed a ruby earring
in front of the bird, hoping he'd take it for
a pomegranate full of seeds –
bite into it and shut up. (16)

Love's chain has broken,
our friendship gone,
mutual respect and affection
wilted
he's just some other dude
strolling down the street.

But my eyes follow him, sweet friend,
I can't help admiring him
day in and day out:
how strange it is
that my heart
hasn't cracked open. (43)

Transcreated from Sanskrit by Gabriel Rosenstock and Abhay K.

SELECTIONS FROM *CHAURASPANCHASIKA*
– Bilhana

Even now
the woodcutter and fisherman turn home,
On his axe the moon and in his dripping net
caught yellow moonlight. The purple flame of fire
calls them to love and sleep. From the hot town
the maker of scant songs for bread wanders
to lie under the clematis flowers with his girl.
The moon shines on her breasts, and I must die . . .

Even now
I mind that I loved cypress and roses, dear,
the great blue mountains and the small grey hills,
the sound of the sea. Upon a day
I saw strange eyes and hands like butterflies;
For me at morning larks flew from the thyme
and children came to bathe in little streams . . .

Even now
I mind that the time of the falling of blossoms
started my dream into a wild life, into my girl;
Then was the essence of her beauty spilled
down on my days so that it fades not,
fails not, subtle and fresh, in perfuming
that day, and the days, and today.

A free interpretation from Sanskrit by E. Powys Mathers

SELECTIONS FROM *GATHASAPTASATI*

Distance destroys love,
So does the lack of it.

Gossip destroys love,
And sometimes

It takes nothing
To destroy love. 81

In her first labour,
She tells her friends,
'I won´t let him
Touch me again.' They laugh. 123

'A scorpion's bitten her,' they cried,
And as she thrashed about,
Her shrewd friends in her husband's presence
Rushed her to her physician lover. 237

Bookish lovemaking
Is soon repetitive.
It's the improvised style
Wins my heart. 274

He groped me
For the underwear
That wasn't
There:

I saw the boy's
Fluster
And embraced him
More tightly. 351

He finds the missionary position
  Tiresome, and grows suspicious
If I suggest another.
  Friend, what's the way out? 476

Translated from Maharashtri Prakrit by Arvind Krishna Mehrotra. The numbers following the poems are according to Albrecht Weber's Das Saptaçatakam des Hāla (Leipzig: F.A. Brockhaus, 1881).

SELECTIONS FROM *THE RIGVEDA* AND *THE UPANISHADAS*

Gayatri Mantra

We meditate
on the glory of that Being
who has produced this universe
May He enlighten our minds.

Translated from Sanskrit by Swami Vivekananda

Pavamāna Mantra
from *Bṛhadāraṇyaka Upaniṣad*

Lead us
from falsehood to truth
from darkness to light
from death to immortality.

Pavamāna: Purification

Shanti Mantra
from *Bṛhadāraṇyaka Upaniṣad*

May all be happy
May all be healthy
May all see the good
May all be free from suffering.

Shanti: Peace

Vasudhaiva Kutumbakam
from *Maha Upanisad*

This is mine, that is yours
narrow-minded people think that way
For the noble-hearted
the whole world is a family.

Vasudhaiva Kutumbakam: The whole world is a family

Translated from Sanskrit by Abhay K.

SELECTION FROM *SADUKTIKARṆĀMṚTA*
– Śrīdharadāsa

She didn't even stop me
by saying, 'Don't leave!'
Nor did she ask -
"would I be away for long?"
She didn't weep long enough
to wet her cheeks
I was ready to depart
when she came
offering me a drink
for the road and placed
a fresh mango blossom
on my palm.
I could not move an inch. (923)

Transcreated from Sanskrit by Gabriel Rosenstock and Abhay K.

SELECTION FROM *ŚĀRṄGADHARAPADDHATI*

– Śārṅgadhara

As the bright day dawns
washing their podiums, they
gossip about politics and the antics
of the other sadhus,
they've been up till midnight
weaving their flowers and grass
for worship rituals.

Later, pretending to practice yoga
and austerities, they hang around
until they catch a glimpse of city girls
gently washing their supple breasts.

Thus these rogues
pass their time
by the river. (4028)

Transcreated from Sanskrit by Gabriel Rosenstock and Abhay K.

SELECTIONS FROM *SUBHĀṢITARATNAKOṢA*

– Silabhattarika

He was the first with whom I lay
and he is my husband now
Oh those moon-drenched nights!
A cooling breeze would come down from the slopes
carrying with it the drunken scent of jasmine.
I am who I was then, and yet I feel my heart
longing for that reed bank on the mountainside
that was witness to our loving and desire . . .
the whole night on fire. (815 | 24.9)

–Silhana

"They are flashes of lightning, sudden, snake-like,
and plunge us into darkness when they are gone.
Therefore let us forego the pleasures of the flesh
and cleave to the perfection of silence . . ."
How we belch out these words in cool, measured tones
shamelessly like foolish parrots:
Reciting, reciting, reciting until kingdom come. (1614 | 48.21)

Transcreated from Sanskrit by Gabriel Rosenstock

SELECTION FROM *SUBHĀṢITĀVALĪ*

– Vallabhadeva

The sun glows
like post-sacrificial embers
and rests a while on the western peaks,
the honeybee is sucked by sweetness
into the lotus, not knowing
the flower will close when light fails.

Those who earn money
with thought of profit only
cannot comprehend
their great loss. (1917)

Transcreated from Sanskrit by Gabriel Rosenstock and Abhay K.

SELECTIONS FROM *THERIGATHA*
– Mutta

Free, fabulously free
free from three trifles –
pounder, pounding bowl and my wicked lord
free from endless births and deaths
the chains that fettered me down
are suddenly no more.

– Sumangalmata

A woman set free at last, how free
how gloriously free I am from drudgery
of kitchen, harsh hunger pangs
the sound of empty pots,
free from that whimsical man
the spinner of yarns
peace at last

lust and hatred have gone
I rest under the shade of sprawling trees
and cherish happiness.

Transcreated from Pali by Abhay K. and Gabriel Rosenstock

SHAPES
– Chokhamela

The sugarcane is crooked
but not its juice.
The bow is curved
not the arrow.
The river is bent
but not its water.
Chokha is twisted
not his faith.
Why are you drawn
to the shape of a thing.

Translated from Marathi by Rohini Mokashi-Punekar

SONG OF THE AVADHUT

– Dattatreya

Truly, it is by the grace of God
that the knowledge of Unity arises within.
Then a man is released at last
from the great fear of life and death.

All that exists in this world of forms
is nothing but the Self, and the Self alone.
How, then, shall the Infinite worship Itself?
Shiva is one undivided Whole!

The five subtle elements that combine to compose this world
are as illusory as the water in a desert mirage;
To whom, then, shall I bow my head?
I, myself, am the stainless One!

Truly, all this universe is only my Self;
It is neither divided nor undivided.
How can I even assert that it exists?
I can only view it with wonder and awe!

What, then, is the heart of the highest truth,
The core of knowledge, the wisdom supreme?
It is, "I am the Self, the formless One;
By my very nature, I am pervading all."

That one God who shines within everything,
who is formless like the cloudless sky,
is the pure, stainless, Self of all.
Without any doubt, that is who I am.

I'm the infinite and immutable One;
I'm pure Consciousness, without any form.
I don't know how, or to whom,
joy and sorrow appear in this world.

Translated from Sanskrit by S. Abhayananda (Stanza 1-7, Ch-1, Avadhut Gita)

SOUL SONG
– Abhay K.

I was always here
as blowing wind
or falling leaves
as shining sun
or flowing streams
as chirping birds
or blooming buds
as blue sky
or empty space
I was never born
I didn't die.

English

SUMMER

from Jayavallabha's *Vajjalagam*

Having burnt it all to ash
along with every animal,
the wild fire
shins up a dried-out tree
and surveys the forest again,
wondering what is left.

Translated from Prakrit by Martha Ann Selby

SUNDORI

– Kynpham Sing Nongkynrih

Beloved Sundori,
Yesterday one of my people
Killed one of your people
And one of your people
Killed one of my people.
Today they have both sworn
To kill on sight.
But this is neither you nor I
Shall we meet by the Umkhrah River
And empty this madness
Into its angry summer floods?
I send this message
Through a fearful night breeze
Please leave your window open.

Translated from Khasi by the poet

THE BLACK MAN

–Ved Pal Deep

When I take a pen and a piece of paper
to collect the thoughts of my mind,
the picture of a black man
rises before my eyes.
His blood is red –

The blood of all humanity.
His thick, tufted and rough locks are
like an intertwined dense forest.
His muscles are strong as trees.
His white teeth produce
thunder and lightning;
At their very sight,
the glory of white civilization crumbles.
When I take up pen to write a verse
it becomes a gun
which a Negro of Congo
hangs on his shoulder,
somewhere in the deep dark wood,
under the cover of a tree,
to fire at the Belgian army.
When I have put down a word
in ink
on a piece of paper,
it becomes
a bright piece of diamond;
Its dusty ores
black hands sift out of deep earth,
underneath rugged plains and rocks,
to deck the crowns
in foreign lands.
When I move my lips

to sing songs,
I feel
tribes after tribes,
countless families of mankind,
like lions,
move out,
break their chains
behind the barbed fences of
the zoo,
built by their foreign masters.

Translated from Dogri by Balraj Puri

THE DAY SHE WAS GONE

– Namdeo Dhasal

The day she was gone,
I painted my face black.
I slapped the savage schizophrenic wind hard in its face.
I picked up small pieces of my life
and stood naked in front of a cracked mirror.
I allowed myself to wreak vengeance upon myself.
I stared condescendingly at the Sun and said, 'You screwball!'
I showered choice curses upon all artists who paint dreams;
I walked from the East towards the West;
I picked stones I found on the way and hurled them at myself,
How boisterously flows this water in its fit of laughter
through mountains and gorges.
What ocean is it seeking to meet?
Or will it seep
into the soil at sea-level?
Did even I belong to myself?
I could not even embrace her dead body
and cry my heart out.
The day she was gone,
I painted my face black.

Translated from Marathi by Dilip Chitre

THE DESCRIPTION OF UMA'S LOVEMAKING

– Kalidasa

Shiva taught her how to make love
in their bed; Parvati offered him back
herself, full of grace of a young woman,
like a present one gives to one's guru

She trembled in pain as her bitten
lower lip was released slowly
Parvati took a deep breath of cool air
coming from the crescent moon in Shiva's hair

While kissing her long hair
dust fell into Shiva's third eye
Parvati blew it off with her perfumed breath
fragrant as the smell of a blossoming lotus

So the lord of the beasts whose mount is Nandi-
the Bull, gratifying Kama, the God of Love
by immersing himself in pleasures of senses
lived for a month with Uma in the Mountain King's palace.

Transcreated from Sanskrit by Abhay K. from Kumarasambhava 8.17-8.20

THE DOOR

– Anamika

I was a door
The harder they beat me
the wider I opened
They walked in and saw
a great cosmic whirling
When the grinding stops, the spinning begins
When the spinning stops, the sewing begins
Something or other, all day, non-stop

And in the end my broom sweeps it all up
sweeps up the stars in the sky
mountains, trees, stones
all the shards and splinters of creation
and collects them in a basket
stores them somewhere
deep inside
in some corner of the mind.

Translated from Hindi by Ritu Menon

THE HERON

– Nannakaiyar

He said, "I am leaving, going away."
And I knew that once again
he was playing games with me.
"Get lost," I snapped at him.
"And don't bother coming back."

But where is he, my lord?
For only he can comfort me.
Tears fill the space between my breasts,
now a vast pond where white herons
with black legs stalk their prey.

Translated from Tamil by R. Parthasarathy

THE LEAF ON THE BRANCH

– Gulzar

It was perched on a branch;
Below were the waters of a lake,
And in it the reflection of the sky;
It was afraid of being drowned
But…
It neither swam, nor drowned, nor flew away
It just sat on the branch, and finally wilted…
One lone leaf on a branch!

Translated from Urdu by Pavan K. Varma

THE MESSENGER SPEAKS TO RADHA

– Jayadeva

Krishna lingers
in the thicket
where together you mastered the secrets
of lovemaking.
Fixed in meditation,
sleepless
he chants a sequences of mantras.
He has one burning desire –
to draw *amrita*
from your offered breasts.

Sighs, short repeated gasps –
he glances around helpless.
The thicket deserted.
He pushes back in, his breath
comes in a rasp.
He rebuilds the couch of blue floral branches.
Steps back and studies it.
Radha, precious Radha!
Your lover turns on a wheel,
image after
feverish image.

She ornaments her limbs
if a single leaf stirs
in the forest.
She thinks it's you, folds back
the bedclothes and stares
in rapture for hours.
Her heart conceives a hundred
amorous games on the well-prepared bed.

But without you
this wisp of a girl
will fade
to nothing tonight . . .

Translated from Sanskrit by Andrew Schelling

THE MAGICIAN

– Kamal Vora

The magician
pulled a rabbit out of his hat
and a dove from his jacket.
An orange appeared in his left hand
with the lost ring hidden inside it.

Whispering something with closed eyes
waving the magic wand,
he offered from his closed palm
whatever was asked for.
With a touch of his fingertips,
the pieces assembled
into a whole
one into two
two into many
Several into one.
What was visible just a second ago
vanished.

Afterwards, the conjuror continued chuckling.

From the crowd
one boy spoke up,
"Magician,
I'm frightened by your magic!
What if you turn me into a butterfly
that flutters away?"

The magician just continued laughing.
Then spreading his arms like wings,
he flew
right through the boy's eyes.

Translated from Gujarati by Dileep Jhaveri and Bill Wolak

THE SEA

– Sitanshu Yashaschandra

I have seen the ocean
before gods and demons simplified it.

I have seen water in the light
of polar submarine fire.
Fire and moisture are one.
To burn and to get wet are one and the same.

When I emerged from the sea
my palms held no pearls.
I am not a diver.
I am a poet.
That which is there, is there in my eyes.

Translated from Gujarati by E.V. Ramakrishnan

THE SECRET
– Joseph Furtado

Every year you blossom, tamarind,
and the sunbirds seek you as of old;
Every day gay children, tamarind,
come to romp around you as of old;
And, lo, every hour of the day
all these years I've waited, tamarind –
Silence! silence to the last, I pray;
It was all so fated, tamarind.
Pride consumes him, said they, tamarind,
And no pity had they, tamarind;
You the secret keep now, tamarind,
Keep it till all secrets are made known,
for I go to sleep now, tamarind,
till o'er all the trumpet's blown.

English

THE TASTE OF IRON

– Dhumil

Look how words
are styled into a poem
Look at this
Read this man fallen amid letters.
You hear that?
Is it the clanging of iron or
the blood spilled on the soil?
Ask not the blacksmith
the taste of iron,
Ask the horse with a leash on his mouth.

Translation from Hindi by Kamalakar Bhat

THE TIGER

– Kavarpentu

"Where is your son?" you ask,
leaning against the fine pillar of my house.
I don't really know where he is.
This womb that bore him is now a desolate cave
a tiger once prowled around.
Go, look for him on the battlefield.

Translated from Tamil by R. Parthasarathy

THE UNICORN
– Suniti Namjoshi

I rode the wild unicorn,
in the green light of trees,
in the dark light of night,
past leaves and silver thorn,
in love and foul weather.
Love, will you ride with me?
But my love stayed behind,
far away behind me.
And I rode the wild unicorn
past love and foul weather.

English

THE YELLOW MUSTARD

– Amir Khusrau

The yellow mustard is blooming in every field,
Mango buds are clicking open, other flowers too;
The koyal chirps from branch to branch,
And the maiden tries her make-up,
The gardener-girls have brought bouquets.
Colourful flowers of all kinds,
in hands everyone's bringing;
But Aashiq-rung, who had promised to come
to Nizamuddin's house in spring,
hasn't turned up - it's been years.

The yellow mustard is blooming in every field.

Aashiq-rung: the lover
Koyal: Cuckoo

Translated from Persian by Anon

THE YOUNG WOMAN WHO SELLS FLOWERS

– Parimal Hansda

That young woman who, standing by the road
was selling flowers, today
She herself has turned into a
very beautiful flower

To suck the nectar of her body
like bumblebees, buzzing around her are so many
young men
Today, her address is
a hidden alley in the market
where, to fight her hunger,
she has turned her body into a shop

That young woman, when she stands at the bus terminus
or walks in the midst of people on the footpath
then, on spotting her, those very young men
avert their eyes and hide
behind the open ends of the saris of their women

That young woman is one of the many young women
And now she is not dependent on anyone anymore
She raises both her hands towards the sky
as if she knows that she would be able to touch and hold
the moving, glowing, blinking stars, planets, constellations

Sari: A garment worn by Indian women

Translated from Santhali by Hansda Sowvendra Shekhar

TIME DOES NOT PASS

– Rajendra Bhandari

Baje has become incapable of going down to the fields
Last year, using a stick, he could reach the yard
This time he only made it to the porch
After a three-day confinement, Baje passed away.
Boju passed away
Then mother began to pass away
At first she passed from the yard to the porch
At the porch she became a scarecrow to the grain
drying in the yard
The light passed from her eyes,
from her legs, the strength to stand
even as her desires were passing,
she passed away herself.
One day, a wild young thing flirted with me
But like a calm lake, I pooled by her side
Youth was passing from me
In the yellow autumn, in the fields
the paddy was passing into haystacks
the grain had passed and become manure
The world itself is passing every day
The atmosphere is passing into the ozone hole
With the passing of seedling, and of plant
the passing of flower and dead leaves
the passing of leaf and shoot
the passing of bud and flower
with these passages
the venerable lotus passed from the face of the earth
But time has not passed
Time is just not there
Time would pass, if at all it existed.

Baje: Grandfather
*Boju:*Grandmother

Translated from Nepali by Anmole Prasad

TRAFFIC JAM

– Nilim Kumar

As I drive out from home
suddenly I forget
where I was headed to
When I get stuck
in traffic jams in a hurry
then I feel restless
and I remember
where I was headed to

Many people tell me –
'I saw you the other day
in the traffic jam'

Yes!
Who was it that saw me in the traffic jam?
I have to enter into another traffic jam
to remember.

Translated from Assamese by Bibekananda Choudhury

WASN'T IT WOMAN WHO BORE THEM

– Sanchiya Honnamma

Wasn't it woman who bore them
Wasn't it woman who raised them
Then why do they always blame woman,
These boors, these blind ones.

In the womb they are the same
When they are growing they are the same
Later the girl will take, with love, what's given
The boy will take his share by force.

For money's sake, for trust
and friendship's sake
Don't give a girl to a walking corpse
bereft of virtue, youth and looks.

Don't say, "We are poor people, where
can we get jewels from?"
Instead of spending on yourself
provide your daughters with clothes and ornaments.

Translated by Tejaswini Niranjana from Kannada

WHEN YOU COME

– Anupama Basumatary

Whenever you come
I stay rooted, still,
a tree standing
mute sculpture.

This hour of meeting you
is bright as day
green as grass.

Yet, sure as death
is our parting.

Translated from Assamese by Pradip Acharya

WHERE THE MIND IS WITHOUT FEAR

– Rabindranath Tagore

Where the mind is without fear and the head is held high
Where knowledge is free
Where the world has not been broken up into fragments
by narrow domestic walls
Where words come out from the depth of truth
Where tireless striving stretches its arms towards perfection
Where the clear stream of reason has not lost its way
into the dreary desert sand of dead habit
Where the mind is led forward by thee
into ever-widening thought and action
Into that heaven of freedom let my country awake.

Translated from Bengali by the poet

WHO WAS IT?

– Shahryar

Who was it, who was it
Who broke the spell of the city of dreams
Who clanged every chord of my soul
Who abandoned me in the arms of emptiness

It wasn't the merciless sky
Nor was it the confidante of my sorrows
It wasn't my poor, frail body
Then who was it?

Translated from Urdu by Rakshanda Jalil

WITHIN
– Basavanna

Say now, what good is it
if a parrot can read aloud
but cannot hear the cat approaching
or if an eye can see the world
not knowing that the eye is squinting?
They say they know the world and all its sin
And fail, O Lord, to look within!

Translated from Kannada by Laxmi Chandrashekar and Vijaya Guttal, reworked by Gabriel Rosenstock

WITHOUT MY BODY

– B.B. Agarwal

When I returned home this evening
a strange incident happened :
nobody noticed me.
My wife did not ask me for tea
my children too kept away from me
my servant, showing great impertinence
kept on cleaning the floor
as if I did not exist.
Well, am I here or not?

Suddenly, then, I realize
with a feeling of great astonishment.
My body is missing.
I want to switch on the radio –
my hands are missing.
I want to speak –
my mouth is gone!
I have vision, alas! no eyes.
I can think – but my head is missing
So...
How have I returned home?

Slowly I started to understand:
I left my mind in the office accidentally while heading home.
My hands still hanging from the bus-strap.
My eyes still scanning the office files;
my mouth stuck to the telephone.
And my feet left standing in a queue, no doubt.
That's how I returned home today, without my body.

Vision of a bodiless life
is the essence of Indian philosophy
But is the exhaustion weighing down the bodiless me
also a part of it all?

Translated from Hindi by Abhay K.

YOU

– Ismail

You're mine
only when you take off all your clothes
for me

When you're dressed
you belong to the world

I'm going to shred this world
into pieces
one day

Translated from Telugu by Velcheru Narayan Rao

YOU AND I

from *Kuruntokai*

My mother and yours, what are they to each other?
my father and yours, how are they kin?
You and I, how do we know each other, and yet somehow
like water raining down on red earth
our loving hearts have mingled.

Translated from Tamil by George L. Hart

YOU CANNOT OWN SOMEONE

– Firaq Gorakhpuri

Nobody has ever belonged to someone for a whole lifetime
You cannot own someone
The beauty that you see with your eyes and the love that you feel
are only the illusions of the mind
All my life I have tried to save myself from
the glances of your eyes
Even then I failed and the dagger went
right through me.

Translated from Urdu by the poet

YOU WOULD HAVE BEEN A SAINT

– Ghalib

Ah, Ghalib, the magic of your words and your ways with mystics!
You would have been a saint – if you were not addicted to drink.

Translated from Urdu by Gulzar

ACKNOWLEDGEMENTS

I would like to thank Gabriel Rosenstock without whose support and encouragement this anthology would not have seen the light of day.

I want to thank Dipanjali for designing a great cover for this anthology. I would like to thank Rajiv Beri, Paul Vinay Kumar, Jyoti Mehrotra, Rajbilochan Prasad and Satyabrat Mishra of Bloomsbury India for their constant support and belief in this book. I wish to thank Shelly Bhoil for carefully going through the text and making valuable suggestions.

I take full responsibility for any error that might have inadvertently crept into the anthology.

PERMISSIONS ACKNOWLEDGMENTS

All the poems included in the anthology have been voluntarily contributed by the poets and/or their respective translators. Permission to include the poems has been granted by the individual poets, translators and publishers. If through inability to trace the present copyright owners, any copyright material is included for which permission has not specifically been sought, apologies are tendered in advance to proprietors and publishers concerned. Every effort has been made to trace individual copyright-holders. This has not been possible for every poem; therefore, the publisher will be happy to make the necessary amendments at the first opportunity.

'This Homage We Pay' (*Uttararāmacarita* of Bhavabhūti 1.1), transcreated from Sanskrit by Gabriel Rosenstock and Abhay K., used by permission of Gabriel Rosenstock and Abhay K.

'A Poem' by Mir Taqui Mir translated by E. Powys Mathers from *The Garden of Bright Waters: One Hundred and Twenty Asiatic Love Poems*. Available in public domain.

'A Poem Never Says Anything' by Uttaran Chaudhuri, translated from Bengali by the poet, used by permission of Uttaran Chaudhuri. First appeared in *The Journal of Poetry Society of India*, Vol. 23, 2012.

'Ambapali' by Vishwanath Prasad Tiwary, translated from Hindi by Sunita Jain, used by permission of Vishwanath Prasad Tiwary and Sunita Jain.

'Amrutlal' by Udayan Thakker, translated from Gujarati by the poet, used by permission of Udayan Thakker.

'Aubade' by R. Parthasarathy, *Kavya Bharati*, 16 (2004). Copyright © 2017 by R. Parthasarathy, used by permission of R. Parthasarathy.

'Aubade' by Jayshankar Prasad, translated from Hindi by Romila Thapar, used by permission of Romila Thapar.

'Bars' by Keki N. Daruwalla, used by permission of Keki N. Daruwalla.

'Black Bag' by Pavankumar Jain, translated from Gujarati by Arvind Krishna Mehrotra; used by permission of Arvind Krishna Mehrotra

'Bone of Time' by Jayanta Mahapatra, used by permission of Jayanta Mahapatra.

'Breasts' by Kutti Revathi, translated from Tamil by Lakshmi Holmström, used by permission of Kutti Revathi, Mark Holmström and Radhika Holmström.

'Breath' (Poem 52) by Lal Ded, translation(c) Ranjit Hoskote from Kashmiri; used by permission of Ranjit Hoskote. First appeared in I, Lalla:The Poems of Lal Ded (New Delhi: Penguin Classics, 2011).

'Champa' by Katyayani, translated from Hindi by Nirupama Dutt, used by permission of Nirupama Dutt.

'Chill Out' by Anon, transcreation by Gabriel Rosenstock and Abhay K., original language: Gondi, used by permission of Gabriel Rosenstock and Abhay K.

'Conversation Piece' by Eunice de Souza, used by permission of Eunice de Souza.

'Dance of Shiva' by Hoshang Merchant, used by permission of Hoshang Merchant.

'Dawn in Winter' by Agyeya, translated from Hindi by Lucy Rosenstein, used by permission of Lucy Rosenstein.

'Death of a Rogue Elephant' by N. N. Kakkad, translated from Malayalam by E.V. Ramakrishnan, used by permission of E.V. Ramakrishnan.

'Description of the Missing One' by Kunwar Narain, translated from Hindi by Apurva Narain, used by permission of Apurva Narain.

'Digamabara' by Anitha Thampi, translated from Malayalam by K. Satchidanandan, used by permission of Anitha Thampi and K. Satchidanandan.

'Easy, Friend' by Kabir, translated from vernacular Hindi by Arvind Krishna Mehrotra, used by permission of Arvind Krishna Mehrotra.

'Engraving of a Bison on Stone' by Arvind Krishna Mehrotra, used by permission of Arvind Krishna Mehrotra.

'Epitaph' by Shakti Chattopadhyay, translated from Bengali by Arvind Krishna Mehrotra, used by permission of Arvind Krishna Mehrotra.

'Epitaph on My Gravestone' by Manushya Puthiran, translated by C.S. Lakshmi and Arundhati Subramaniam, used by permission of Manushya Puthiran, C.S. Lakshmi and Arundhati Subramaniam.

'Every Land Our Home' by Kaniyan Punkunran, Weber Studies 15.1 (Winter 1998), translated from Tamil by R. Parthasarathy,

Copyright © 2017 by R. Parthasarathy, used by permission of R. Parthasarathy

'Famine and After' by Nagarjuna, translated from Hindi by Nalini Taneja, used by permission of Nalini Taneja.

'Father Returning Home' by Dilip Chitre, translated from Marathi by the poet. Used by permission of Vijaya Chitre.

'Four Haiku and a Tanka' by K. Ramesh, used by permission of K. Ramesh.

'Friends, This Is the Only Way' by Sachal Sarmast, translated from Sindhi by Ivan M. Granger, used by permission of Ivan M. Granger.

'Giant Buildings' by Munibur Rahman, transcreation by Gabriel Rosenstock and Abhay K., original language: Urdu, used by permission of Gabriel Rosenstock and Abhay K.

'Grandfather's Photograph' by Mangalesh Dabral, translated from Hindi by Arvind Krishna Mehrotra, used by permission of Mangalesh Dabral and Arvind Krishna Mehrotra.

'He Is a Poet' by Shankar Ramani, translated from Konkani by Damodar Mauzo, used by permission of Damodar Mauzo.

'He Promised He'd Return Tomorrow' by Vidyapati, translated from Maithali by Azfar Hussain, used by permission of Azfar Hussain.

'Horse Play' by K. Ayyappa Paniker, translated from Malayalam by K. Satchidanandan, used by permission of K. Satchidanandan.

'How to Go to the Tao Temple' by K. Satchidanandan, translated from Malayalam by the poet, used with the permission of K. Satchidanandan.

'How to Read a Book' by Muddupalani, translated from Telugu by Velcheru Narayan Rao and David Shulman, used by permission of Velcheru Narayan Rao and David Shulman.

'How to Tame a Pair of New Chappals' by Gopal Honnalgere. Internodes, Samkaleen Prakashan, 1986.

'I Have Given Birth to a Son' (Tribal birth song by a Bhil mother), translated from Bhili by Abraham Thuruthumalil, *Dharmaram Journals, Poetry of Indian Tribals*, Volume 17, Issue 2.

'In Her Lovemaking She Grieves' by Gagan Gill, translated from Hindi by J.P. Das, Arlene Zide and Madhu B. Joshi, used by permission of Gagan Gill, J.P. Das and Arlene Zide.

'Kabariwala' by Kavita A. Jindal, used by permission of Kavita A. Jindal.

'Kalli' by Ajmer Rode, translated from Punjabi by the poet, first published at Poetry International Web, Rotterdam, used by permission of Ajmer Rode.

'Lamination' by Shefali Debbarma, translated from Kokborok by Saroj Chaudhuri, reworked by Abhay K., used by permission of Shefali Debbarma, Saroj Chaudhuri and Abhay K.

'Love Song' by Nirala, translated from Hindi by Arvind Krishna Mehrotra, used by permission of Arvind Krishna Mehrotra.

'Magadh' by Srikant Verma, translated from Hindi by Mrinal Pande, used by permission of Mrinal Pande.

'Making a Chair' by Dileep Jhaveri, used by permission of Dileep Jhaveri.

'Married Love' by Srinivas Rayaprol, used by permission of Aparna Rayaprol

'Moment' by Kaifi Azami, translated from Urdu by Pavan K. Varma, used by permission of Pavan K. Varma.

'Monsoon Clouds Be My Messenger' by Andal, translated from Old Tamil by Priya Sarukkai Chhabria, used by permission of Priya Sarukkai Chhabria.

'Mother Tongue' by Kedarnath Singh, translated from Hindi by Kalpana Singh-Chitnis, used by permission of Kedarnath Singh and Kalpana Singh-Chitnis.

'My Poem' by Surjit Patar, translated from Punjabi by Nirupama Dutt, used by permission of Surjit Patar and Nirupama Dutt.

'Not Entirely Hidden' from *Cātu* verses, translated from Telugu by Velcheru Narayana Rao and David Shulman, used by permission of Velcheru Narayana Rao and David Shulman.

'O My Friends' by Mirabai, transcreation (c) Jane Hirshfield; used by permission of Jane Hirshfield. First appeared in Women in Praise of the Sacred: 43 Centuries of Spiritual Poetry by Women, ed. by Jane Hirshfield (NY: HarperCollins, 1994) and Mirabai: Ecstatic Poems, ed. by Robert Bly and Jane Hirshfield (Boston: Beacon Press, 2004).

'O Sakhi, the Flute Plays in the Grove' by Salabega, translated from Oriya by Sachidanand Mohanty and Smita Mohanty, used by permission of Sachidanand Mohanty.

'Pataliputra' by Patumarattu Mocikiranar, Indian Literature, 39.1 (January-February 1996) translated from Tamil by R. Parthasarathy, copyright © 2017 by R. Parthasarathy, used by permission of R. Parthasarathy.

'Paths' by Salma, translated from Tamil by Lakshmi Holmström, used by permission of Salma, Mark Holmström and Radhika Holmström.

'Pedru Uncle' by Hemant Divate, translated from Marathi by Dilip Chitre, used by permission of Hemant Divate and Vijaya Chitre.

'People' by Tukaram, translated from Marathi by Anon.

'Play' by Ashok Vajpeyi, translated from Hindi by Sudeep Sen, used by permission of Ashok Vajpeyi and Sudeep Sen.

'Praise Galore to the Land of Dhat' by Rangrelo Bithu, translated from Rajasthani by Kesari Singh.

'Pundarīka' by Kshemendra, translated from Sanskrit by W.S. Merwin and J.M. Masson, used by permission of J.M. Masson.

Selections from *Amaruśataka*, transcreated from Sanskrit by Gabriel Rosenstock and Abhay K., used by permission of Gabriel Rosenstock and Abhay K.

Selections from *Chauraspanchasika* by Bilhana, a free interpretation of the *Chauraspanchasika* (Sanskrit) by E. Powys Mathers. Available in public domain.

Selections from *Gathasaptasati*, translated from Maharashtri Prakrit by Arvind Krishna Mehrotra. The numbers following the poems are according to Albrecht Weber's Das Saptacatakam des Hala (Leipzig: F.A. Brockhaus, 1881). Used by permission of Arvind Krishna Mehrotra.

Selections from *The Rigveda and The Upanishadas* – 'Gayatri Mantra' translated from Sanskrit by Swami Vivekananda, available in public domain; 'Pavamāna Mantra' (from *Bṛhadāraṇyaka Upaniṣad*), 'Shanti Mantra' (from *Bṛhadāraṇyaka Upaniṣad*), 'Vasudhaiva Kutumbakam' (From *Maha Upanisad*), translated from Sanskrit by Abhay K., used by permission of Abhay K.

Selection from *Saduktikarṇāmṛta* by Śrīdharadāsa, transcreated from Sanskrit by Gabriel Rosenstock and Abhay K., used by permission of Gabriel Rosenstock and Abhay K.

Selection from *Śārṅgadharapaddhati* by Śārṅgadhara, transcreated from Sanskrit by Gabriel Rosenstock and Abhay K., used by permission of Gabriel Rosenstock and Abhay K.

Selections from *Subhāṣitaratnakoṣa* 815 (24.9) by Silabhattarika and 1614 (48.21) by Śilhana, transcreated from Sanskrit by Gabriel Rosenstock, used by permission of Gabriel Rosenstock.

Selection from *Subhāṣitāvalī* by Vallabhadeva, transcreated from Sanskrit by Gabriel Rosenstock and Abhay K., used by permission of Gabriel Rosenstock and Abhay K.

Selections from *Therigatha*, poems of Mutta and Sumangalmata, transcreation by Abhay K. and Gabriel Rosenstock, original language: Pali, used by permission of Abhay K. and Gabriel Rosenstock.

'Shapes' by Chokhamela, translated from Marathi by Rohini Mokashi-Punekar, used by permission of Rohini Mokashi-Punekar.

'Song of the Avadhut' by Dattatreya, translated from Sanskrit by S. Abhayananda, used by permission of S. Abhayananda.

'Soul Song' by Abhay K., used by permission of Abhay K.

'Summer' from *Vajjalagam* of Jayabhallava, translated from Prakrit by Martha Ann Selby, used by permission of Martha Ann Selby.

'Sundori' by Kynpham Sing Nongkynrih, translated from Khasi by the poet, used by permission of Kynpham Sing Nongkynrih.

'The Black Man' by Ved Pal Deep, translated from Dogri by Balraj Puri.

'The Day She Was Gone' by Namdeo Dhasal, translated from Marathi by Dilip Chitre. Used by permission of Vijaya Chitre.

'The Description of Uma's Lovemaking' by Kalidasa, transcreated from Sanskrit by Abhay K., used by permission of Abhay K.

'The Door' by Anamika, translated from Hindi by Ritu Menon, used by permission of Anamika.

'The Heron' by Nannakaiyar, *Modern Poetry in Translation*, New Series, 9 (Summer 1996), translated from Tamil by R. Parthasarathy. Copyright © 2017 by R. Parthasarathy, used by permission of R. Parthasarathy.

'The Leaf on the Branch' by Gulzar, translated from Urdu by Pavan K. Varma, used by permission of Gulzar and Pavan K. Varma.

'The Magician' by Kamal Vora, translated from Gujarati by Dileep Jhaveri and Bill Wolak, used by permission of Kamal Vora, Dileep Jhaveri and Bill Wolak.

'The Messenger Speaks to Radha' by Jayadeva, translated by Andrew Schelling (from *The Gita-govinda* in Kamini: Poems from Jayadeva's *Gita-govinda*—emdash editions: St. Louis, 2007), used by permission of Andrew Schelling.

'The Sea' by Sitanshu Yashaschandra, translated from by E.V. Ramakrishnan, used by permission of Sitanshu Yashaschandra and E.V. Ramakrishnan.

'The Secret' by Joseph Furtado. Available in public domain.

'The Taste of Iron' by Dhumil, translated from Hindi by Kamalakar Bhat, used by permission of Kamalakar Bhat.

'The Tiger' by Kavarpentu (*Purananuru 86*), *Modern Poetry in Translation*, New Series, 9 (Summer 1996). Translated from Tamil by R. Parthasarathy. Copyright © 2017 by R. Parthasarathy, used by permission of R. Parthasarathy.

'The Unicorn' by Suniti Namjoshi from *Poems* (Writers' Workshop, 1967), used by permission of Suniti Namjoshi.

'The Yellow Mustard' by Amir Khusrau, translated by Anon, available in public domain.

'The Young Woman Who Sells Flowers' by Parimal Hansda, translated from Santhali by Hansda Sowvendra Shekhar, used by permission of Parimal Hansda and Hansda Sowvendra Shekhar.

'Time Does Not Pass' by Rajendra Bhandari, translated from Nepali by Anmole Prasad, used by permission of Rajendra Bhandari and Anmole Prasad.

'Traffic Jam' by Nilim Kumar, translated from Assamese by Bibekanand Choudhury, used by permission of Nilim Kumar.

'Wasn't It Woman Who Bore Them' by Sanchiya Honnamma, translated from Kannada by Tejaswini Niranjana, used by permission of Tejaswini Niranjana.

'When You Come' by Anupama Basumatary, translated from Assamese by Pradip Acharya, used by permission of Anupama Basumatary.

'Where the Mind Is Without Fear' by Rabindranath Tagore, translated from Bengali by the poet, available in public domain.

'Who Was It' by Shahryar, translated from Urdu by Rakhshanda Jalil, used by permission of Rakhshanda Jalil

'Within' by Basavanna, translated from Kannada by Laxmi Chandrashekar and Vijaya Guttal, reworked by Gabriel Rosenstock, used by permission of Laxmi Chandrashekar , Vijaya Guttal and Gabriel Rosenstock.

'Without My Body' by B.B. Agarwal, translated from Hindi by Abhay K., used by permission of Abhay K.

'You' by Ismail, translated from Telugu by Velcheru Narayan Rao, used by permission of Velcheru Narayan Rao.

'You and I' (*Kuruntokai 40*), translated from Tamil by George L. Hart, used by permission of George L. Hart.

'You Cannot Own Someone' by Firaq Gorakhpuri, translated from Urdu by the poet.

'You Would Have Been a Saint' by Ghalib, translated from Urdu by Gulzar, used by permission of Gulzar.

POETS' BIO-NOTES

Abhay K. (b.1980) has published six collections of poems including *The Seduction of Delhi* (Bloomsbury India) and *The Eight-Eyed Lord of Kathmandu* (The Onslaught Press, UK). He is the editor of *CAPITALS* (Bloomsbury India) and *100 Great Indian Poems* (Bloomsbury India). He received the SAARC Literature Award 2013.

Agyeya is the pen name of Sachchidananda Hirananda Vatsyayan (1911–1987). He introduced modern trends in Hindi poetry, fiction, criticism and journalism. He was an exponent of the literary movements *Nayi Kavita* (New Poetry) and *Prayog* (Experiments) in Modern Hindi literature.

Ajmer Rode (b.1940) is a poet, playwright and translator with five volumes of poetry to his credit. He lives in Canada and writes in Punjabi and English.

Amir Khusrau (1253-1325) is a Sufi musician, poet and scholar. He is an iconic figure in the cultural history of the Indian subcontinent. He was a mystic and a spiritual disciple of Nizamuddin Auliya of Delhi. He wrote poetry primarily in Persian, but also in Hindavi.

Anamika (b. 1961) is a contemporary Hindi poet, social worker and novelist from Bihar. She also writes literary criticism in English.

Andal is the only woman among the twelve Alvar saints of South India affiliated to the Srivaishnava tradition of Hinduism. Active in the 7-8th century, she is credited with the great Tamil works *Thiruppavai* and *Nachiar Tirumozhi*.

Anitha Thampi (b. 1968) writes in Malayalam and has published two poetry collections. Her poems have been translated into several languages.

Anupama Basumatary (b.1961) has five collections of poetry and a book of translation to her credit. She received the Bharatiya Bhasha Parishad's Ishan Award for her book *Rupali Ratir Ghat*.

Arvind Krishna Mehrotra (b.1947) is a poet, anthologist, literary critic and translator. He is widely recognized for expanding the Indian English language poetry tradition, established by figures such as A.K. Ramanujan, Nissim Ezekiel, Dom Moraes and Arun Kolatkar.

Ashok Vajpeyi (b. 1941) is a poet, essayist, literary and cultural critic. He writes in Hindi. He has published 23 books of poetry, criticism and art. He received Sahitya Akademi Award in 1994.

Basavanna is a 12th century Hindu philosopher, statesman, Kannada poet in the Shiva-focused Bhakti movement and a social reformer. He is known to have spread social awareness through his *Vachanas*, a specific rhythmic writing in Kannada.

B.B. Agarwal (1919–1975) is an important figure in *Pragativad* movement of Hindi poetry. He published nine collections of poetry and was awarded Sahitya Akademi Award posthumously.

Bhavabhuti is an 8th century scholar of India, noted for his plays and poetry, written in Sanskrit. His play *Malati Madhava* is considered a masterpiece in Sanskrit literature.

Bilhana is an 11th century Kashmiri poet. He is known for his love poem, the *Chauraspanchasika* or *The Love Thief*.

Chokhamela is one of the first Dalit poets of India from the 14th century. He is revered as a saint in Maharashtra. He belonged to the Mahar caste, which was considered untouchable in that era. He wrote many *Abhangas*, a form of devotional poetry sung in the praise of god Vitthala/Vithoba.

Dattatreya is a poet who is also considered as an incarnation of the Divine Trinity – Brahma, Vishnu and Shiva – in Hindu mythology.

Dileep Jhaveri (b. 1943) is a Gujarati language poet, translator, playwright, editor and physician from Mumbai. He has published three poetry collections in Gujarati and has edited an anthology of contemporary Gujarati poetry in English translation entitled *Breath Becoming a Word*.

Dilip Chitre (1938–2009) is one of the foremost poets and critics to emerge in the post-independence period of India. Apart from being a very important bilingual writer in Marathi and English, he was also a painter and filmmaker.

Dhumil (1936–1975) is a renowned Hindi poet from Varanasi, who is known for his revolutionary writings and "protest poetry". His posthumously released second collection of poems earned him Sahitya Akademi Award in 1979.

Eunice de Souza (1940–2017) is an English language poet, literary critic and novelist. Among her notable books of poetry are *Fix* and *Women in Dutch Painting* (1988).

Firaq Gorakhpuri (1896–1982) is the pen name of Raghupati Sahay, a writer, critic and one of the most noted contemporary Urdu poets from India. He received Jnanpith Award in 1969 for his magnum opus *Gul-e-Naghma*.

Ghalib (1797–1869) is the pen name of Mirza Asadullah Beg Khan. He was a preeminent Urdu and Persian-language poet during the last years of the Mughal Empire.

Gagan Gill (b. 1959) has published four collections of poetry. She has also published ten volumes of translations.

Gopal Honnalgere (1942–2003) is a prominent Indian English poet with six poetry collections to his credit.

Gulzar (b. 1934) is the pen name of Sampooran Singh Kalra. He is a well-known poet, lyricist and film director. He received the Sahitya Akademi Award in 2002 for his short stories collection *Dhuan*.

Hemant Divate (b. 1967) is a reputed Marathi poet, editor, translator and publisher based in Mumbai. He has published several poetry collections.

Hoshang Merchant (b. 1947) is a poet based in Hyderabad who writes in English. He has written 20 books of poetry, and four critical studies. He edited India's first gay anthology *Yaraana: Gay Writing from India*.

Jayadeva (1170–1245) is a Sanskrit poet known for his epic poem *Gita Govinda* which concentrates on Krishna's love with Radha in spring season.

Jayanta Mahapatra (b. 1928) is one of the best known contemporary poets and the first ever Indian poet to win the Sahitya Akademi award for English poetry.

Jayavallabha is an 8th century Jain monk. He is known for compiling *Vajjalagan*, a collection of verses in Prakrit.

Joseph Furtado (1872–1947) is a poet and novelist who wrote in the English language. Considered one of the best poets of Goa during his time, he is largely forgotten now.

Kabir is a 15th century mystic poet and saint. He ranks among the world's greatest poets. His writings influenced the Bhakti movement and his verses are found in Sikhism's scripture *Adi Granth*.

Kaifi Azami (1919–2002) is the pen name of Sayyid Akhtar Hussein Rizvi, a renowned Urdu poet and lyricist. He received the Sahitya Akademi Award in 1975 for his poetry collection *Awara Sajde*.

Kamal Vora (b. 1950) is a Gujarati language poet and editor from Mumbai. He is the editor of *Etad*, a quarterly Guajarati literary magazine. He received the Sahitya Akademi Award in 2016.

Kaniyan Punkunran (1st–3rd Century CE) is an influential Tamil poet and philosopher of the Sangam age.

Kalidasa is a 5th century classical Sanskrit writer, widely regarded as the greatest poet and dramatist in the Sanskrit language. His plays and poetry are primarily based on the *Puranas*.

Katyayani (b. 1959) is a poet, activist and publisher. She has published four collections of poems. Some of her poems have been translated into Russian and English.

Kavita A. Jindal (b. 1964) is the author of the poetry collection, *Raincheck Renewed*, published by Chameleon Press to critical acclaim. She has also published fiction, essays and reviews in newspapers and anthologies around the world.

K. Ayyappa Paniker (1930–2006) is an influential Malayalam poet, literary critic, and an academic and a scholar. He is one of the pioneers of modernism in Malayalam poetry.

Kedarnath Singh (b. 1934) is a poet, critic and essayist. He writes in Hindi. He was awarded India's highest literary award Jnanpith in 2013 and Sahitya Akademi Award in 1989.

Keki N. Daruwalla (b. 1937) is a poet and a short story writer in English. He was awarded Sahitya Akademi Award in 1984 for his poetry collection, *The Keeper of the Dead* and Commonwealth Prize for Asia for *Landscapes* in 1987.

K. Ramesh (b. 1966) writes haiku, tanka and free verse. His poems have appeared in several journals that cater to free verse and Japanese forms of poetry.

K. Satchidanandan (b.1928) is a poet and critic. A pioneer of modern poetry in Malayalam, a bilingual literary critic, playwright, editor, columnist and translator, he writes in Malayalam and translates his poems into English.

Kshemendra (c. 990 – c. 1070 CE) is a Sanskrit poet from Kashmir. Around eighteen of his works are still extant while fourteen more are known only through references in other literature.

Kunwar Narain (b. 1927) writes in Hindi. Widely translated, his many honours include Sahitya Akademi Award, Italy's Premio Feronia, Warsaw University's honorary medal, Padma Bhushan and Jnanpith.

Kutti Revathi (b. 1974) is a lyricist, poet, activist and a doctor. She has published three books of poetry and is the editor of *Panikkudam*, a literary quarterly for women's writing.

Kynpham Sing Nongkynrih (b.1964) is a poet, translator and editor from northeast India. His poetry has been widely published in national and international journals. He writes in Khasi and English.

Lal Ded (1320–1392), known as Lalla, was a mystic. Her verses are the earliest compositions in Kashmiri language and are an important part in history of modern Kashmiri literature.

Mangalesh Dabral (b. 1948) is a contemporary poet who writes in Hindi. He has published several collections of poetry and received the Sahitya Akademi Award in 2000.

Manushya Puthiran (b. 1968) is the pen name of Tamil poet S. Abdul Hameed. He has several poetry collections to his credit.

Mirabai is a 16th century Hindu mystic poet and devotee of Krishna. She is a celebrated Bhakti saint, particularly in the North Indian Hindu tradition.

Mir Taqi Mir (1725–1810) was the leading Urdu poet of his time and one of the pioneers of the Urdu language. He was one of the key poets of the Delhi School of the Urdu ghazal.

Mohammad Ismail (1928–2003) is a Telugu-language poet and critic. He was also an academic and university administrator. He wrote more than a dozen books including poetry, criticism and translations.

Muddupalani is an 18th century poet and courtesan. Her main works are the erotic epic *Rādhikā-sāntvanam* besides *Ashtapadi*, a Telugu translation of Jayadeva's eponymous work.

Munibur Rahman (b. 1924) has published nine books, including four poetry collections, beside several articles in scholarly journals. He lives in Michigan.

Mutta was an elder nun active around 600 BCE who contributed poems to one of first poetry anthologies in the world titled *Therigatha*.

Nagarjuna (1911–1998) is the pen name of Vaidya Nath Mishra. He was a Hindi and Maithili poet, known as *Janakavi* – the People's Poet. He received the Sahitya Akademi Award in 1969.

Namdeo Dhasal (1949–2014) is a Marathi poet, writer and Dalit activist from Maharashtra, India. He won a Lifetime Achievement Award from the Sahitya Akademi in 2004.

Nannakaiyar (1st–3rd Century CE) is a Sangam era Tamil language poet.

Nilim Kumar (b. 1961) has seventeen poetry collections and three novels to his credit. He writes in Assamese. His poems have been translated into several languages.

Nirala (1896-1961) [Suryakant Tripathi 'Nirala'] is a poet, novelist, essayist and story-writer and a prominent figure in modern Hindi literature.

N. N. Kakkad (1927–1987) is a poet in Malayalam language. He was a Sanskrit scholar as well as a broadcaster.

Parimal Hansda (b. 1986) is a poet in Santhali language. He has published an anthology of poems and a collection of short stories.

Pavankumar Jain (1947–2013) wrote in both English and Gujarati. His first collection of Gujarati poems, *Pasath Kavyo* (Sixty five poems), appeared in 2012.

Patumarattu Mocikiranar (1st–3rd Century CE) is a Sangam era Tamil language poet.

Rabindranath Tagore (1861–1941) is the author of *Gitanjali*. He won the Nobel Prize in Literature in 1913.

Rajendra Bhandari (b. 1956) is a poet in Nepali. He has published several collections of poems.

Rangrelo Bithu is a poet from Jaisalmer, Rajasthan who wrote in Rajasthani.

R. Parthasarathy (b. 1934) is a poet, translator, and editor. He is best known for his long poem, *Rough Passage* (Oxford University Press, 1977). His translation of the Tamil epic, *The Tale of an Anklet* (Columbia University Press, 1993), received the Sahitya Akademi award in 1996.

Sachal Sarmast (1739–1827) is the penname of Abdul Wahab Farouqi, a Sufi poet from Sindh. He wrote poetry in several languages, most prominently in Sindhi.

Shahryar (1936–2012) is a renowned poet and lyricist who was also an academician. He wrote in Urdu. He received the Sahitya Akademi Award in 1987 and Jnanpith in 2008.

Salabega is a 17th century poet from Odisha. He occupies a permanent position among the devotional poets of Odisha for devoting his life to Lord Jagannath.

Salma (b. 1968) is a well-known name in contemporary Tamil

literature. A poet, novelist and political activist, she has published two collections of poems, short fiction and novels.

Śārṅgadhara is the 14th century compiler of Śārṅgadharapaddhati, a Sanskrit anthology (1363 CE) which has 4689 poetic verses divided into 163 sections (*paddhati*).

Shakti Chattopadhyay (1933–1995) is a poet and writer in Bengali. He received the Sahitya Akademi Award in 1983.

Shankar Ramani (b. 1923) is a Goan poet felicitated with Sahitya Academy award for his poetry collection in Konkani in 1996.

Shefali Debbarma (b. 1964) is poet from Tripura, northeast India. She writes in Kokborok. She received Tripura State Award for poetry in 2004.

Silabhattarika is a poet from ancient India known for grace and ease of her poetic style.

Silhana is a poet from Kashmir. His *Shantisataka* is quoted in *Saduktikarnamrta* which was composed in 1205 CE.

Sitanshu Yashaschandra (b. 1941) is a Gujarati poet, playwright, translator and academic. He received the Sahitya Akademi Award in 1987 and Padma Shri in 2006.

Śrīdharadāsa is a 12th century poet and compiler of Saduktikarṇāmṛta. He was active at the Sena court and is the author of various works in Sanskrit.

Srikant Verma (1931–1986) is a poet and the author of twenty books. He was also a politician. He was given the Sahitya Akademi Award posthumously for *Magadh*.

Srinivas Rayaprol (1925–1998) is a prominent Indian English poet. He also translated Telugu poetry into English. Three anthologies of his poetry were published by Writers Workshop, Kolkata.

Sumangalmata was an elder nun who lived around 600 BCE and contributed poems to one of first poetry anthologies in the world titled *Therigatha*.

Suniti Namjoshi (b. 1941) is a poet and a fabulist. She has written many collections of fables and poetry, several novels, and more than a dozen children's books. Her work has been translated into several languages.

Surjit Patar (b. 1945) is a Punjabi language poet. He received the Sahitya Akademi Award in 1993.

Tukaram is a 17th century poet-saint from Maharashtra, India. He is best known for his Abhanga, a form of devotional poetry sung in praise of the Hindu god Vitthala.

Udayan Thakker (b. 1955) is a Gujarati language poet, writer and translator from Mumbai, India.

Uttaran Chaudhuri (b. 1982) is a poet in Bengali. He works as a creative supervisor in an advertising firm in Kolkata. His poems have appeared in several literary magazines.

Vallabhadeva is a Sanskrit poet from the 16th century. He is one of the compliers of Subhasitavali.

Ved Pal Deep (1929–1995) is a poet and translator. He wrote both in Hindi and Dogri.

Vidyapati (1352–1448) is a writer from Bihar who has written in Mathili and Sanskrit. His poetry influenced Bengali, Maithili, and other Eastern literary traditions.

Vishwanath Prasad Tiwary (b. 1940) is a Hindi poet and critic. He has written a number of poetry books. He is currently the President of Sahitya Akademi, the National Academy of Letters.

TRANSLATORS' BIO-NOTES

Abraham Thuruthumalil is a translator from Indian tribal languages.

Andrew Schelling is a poet, eco-activist, and translator from Sanskrit. He is the author of twenty odd books and teaches at Naropa University.

Anmole Prasad is a poet and translator. He translates from Nepali into English.

Apurva Narain translates from Hindi. His translations have been published in leading literary journals.

Arlene Zide is a poet and translator based in New York. She translates from Hindi and Urdu.

Arundhati Subramaniam is an award-winning poet and writer on spirituality and culture.

Balraj Puri (1928-2014) was a prolific writer in English as well as Urdu and Hindi. He was also a well-known journalist and human rights activist.

Bill Wolak is an American poet and translator. He teaches creative writing at William Paterson University in New Jersey.

Bibekanand Chaudhury is a noted translator of languages from the northeast India.

C.S. Lakshmi is a writer and researcher. She writes under the pseudonym Ambai.

David Shulman is an Indologist and regarded as one of the world's foremost authorities on the languages of India.

E. Powys Mathers (1892-1939) was an English translator and poet, known for his translation of *Asian Love Poems* and *One Thousand and One Nights*.

E.V. Ramakrishnan is a bilingual writer and translator. He has published poetry and literary criticism in his mother tongue Malayalam and in English.

Gabriel Rosenstock is a poet, tankaist, haikuist, novelist, essayist, playwright, author/translator of over 180 books, mostly in Irish (Gaelic).

George L. Hart is a professor of Tamil language at the University of California, Berkeley.

Hansda Sowvendra Shekhar is the author of two books. He translates from Santhali and Hindi into English.

Ivan M. Granger is the founder and editor of the Poetry Chaikhana, a publishing house and an online resource for sacred poetry from around the world.

Jane Hirshfield is an award-winning American poet, essayist, and translator and author of several poetry collections.

J.S. Masson is an American author and translator. His translations of Sanskrit poems have received praise.

Kalpna Singh-Chitnis is an award-winning poet and translator. She translates from Hindi into English and vice versa. Her translated works have appeared in notable journals.

Kamalakar Bhat is a bilingual writer and a translator between Kannada and English. He has translated poetry by several contemporary Kannada poets.

Kesari Singh is a translator of *Dingal* (Rajasthani) poetry into English. He is the editor of *An Anthology of Rajasthan Poetry*. He is also a politician and belongs to *Charan* community.

Laxmi Chandrashekhar is a prolific translator from Kannada into English.

Lakshmi Holmström (1935-2016) is a noted writer, literary critic and translator from Tamil.

Lucy Rosenstein teaches Hindi at SOAS, University of London. She grew up in Bulgaria.

Martha Ann Selby is an associate professor of South Asian studies in the Department of Asian Studies at the University of Texas at Austin, where she teaches courses on Indian literature.

Nalini Taneja is a professor at Delhi University. She translates from Hindi into English.

Nirupama Dutt is a poet, translator, author and literary/art critic based in Chandigarh. Her latest translation includes Gulzar's short poetry collection Pluto.

Pavan K. Varma is a writer, translator, politician and former diplomat. He has authored several books.

Pradip Acharya has taught at Cotton College in Guwahati and is a prolific translator in Assamese and English.

Rakhsnanda Jalil is a writer, critic and literary historian. She has published over 15 books. She is presently writing a biography of Shahryar.

Ranjit Hoskote is a poet, cultural theorist and curator. He has authored 30 books. He was honoured with the Sahitya Akademi Award for translation.

Ritu Menon is a writer and publisher. She co-founded Kali for Women, India's first feminist publishing house.

Rohini Mokeshi-Punekar is professor of English at the Indian Institute of Technology, Guwahati.

Romila Thapar is a historian and author of several books. She has also translated some poetry, published in Poetry Chicago.

S. Abhayananda was born as Stanley Ross Trout in 1938 in Indianapolis, Indiana. He has authored and translated a number of books on spirituality including *The Avadhut Gita*.

Sachidanand Mohanty is a professor and Vice Chancellor of the Central University of Orissa, Koraput.

Saroj Chaudhury is a poet, academician and translator from tribal languages of North East India.

Sudeep Sen is a poet, editor and translator. His translations have featured in several reputed literary journals. He received A.K. Ramanujan Translation Award in 2009.

Sunita Jain is a scholar, novelist, short-story writer and poet of English and Hindi literature.

Tejaswini Niranjana is a professor, cultural theorist, translator and author.

Velcheru Narayan Rao is currently professor of Telugu Culture, Literature and History at Emory University, Atlanta, Georgia.

Vijaya Guttal is a retired professor of English from Karnatak University, Dharwad.

W.S. Merwin is a leading American writer whose poetry, translations, and prose have received accolades.

Disclaimer: Wikipedia is the principal source of the bio-notes of the late poets and translators included in this anthology. The bio-notes of most of the living poets and translators are provided by themselves.

POETS INDEX